the Universe

DK

DK | Penguin
Random
House

Author Abigail Beall
Illustrator Dawn Cooper
Subject Consultant Sophie Allan
Project Editors Clare Lloyd, Kat Teece
Senior Art Editor Rachael Parfitt Hunt
Editor Phil Hunt
US Editor Jane Perlmutter
US Senior Editor Shannon Beatty
Designer Sunita Gahir
Jacket Designer Sunita Gahir
Jacket Coordinator Elin Woosnam
Project Picture Researcher Rituraj Singh
Picture Researcher Ridhima Sikka
Production Editor Dragana Puvacic
Production Controller Rebecca Parton
Managing Editor Penny Smith
Deputy Art Director Mabel Chan
Publishing Director Sarah Larter

First American Edition, 2024
Published in the United States by DK Publishing,
a division of Penguin Random House LLC
1745 Broadway, 20th Floor, New York, NY 10019

Copyright © 2024 Dorling Kindersley Limited
A Penguin Random House Company
24 25 26 27 28 10 9 8 7 6 5 4 3 2 1
001–342147–Nov/2024

A catalog record for this book
is available from the Library of Congress.
ISBN: 978-0-5938-4365-9

DK books are available at special discounts when purchased
in bulk for sales promotions, premiums, fund-raising,
or educational use.
For details, contact: DK Publishing Special Markets,
1745 Broadway, 20th Floor, New York, York, NY 10019
SpecialSales@dk.com

Printed and bound in China

www.dk.com

MIX
Paper | Supporting
responsible forestry
FSC™ C018179

This book was made with Forest
Stewardship Council™ certified paper –
one small step in DK's commitment to a
sustainable future. For more information
go to www.dk.com/our-green-pledge

Contents

WELCOME TO THE UNIVERSE

The universe is the name we use to describe everything we know to exist. It includes Earth, all the planets, all the stars, galaxies, black holes and much, much more. It is bigger than we can ever imagine.

Earth is part of the solar system—eight planets that orbit a star called the sun. In our galaxy, the Milky Way, there are billions of other stars. And in the universe, there are billions of other galaxies, each with its own stars and planets. There are also invisible parts to the universe, including mysterious stuff called dark matter and a force called dark energy. We don't know what they are made of, we just know they exist. We use powerful telescopes to explore the most distant, and youngest, galaxies to tell us about the universe.

Asteroids

Dwarf planets

Planets

The universe is made up of asteroids, dwarf planets, planets, nebulae, stars, galaxies, and more...

In this book, we will learn what the universe is made of, what it is like on planets orbiting other stars, and what scientists can piece together about parts of the universe we can't directly see.

We will discover how to navigate our way around the night sky using patterns of stars, and we will meet people who have done more than just navigate with their imaginations—astronauts who have been into space themselves.

So turn the page to begin exploring the marvels and mysteries of the universe, from the moment it all began with the big bang, through how stars and planets formed, and on to the universe we see today.

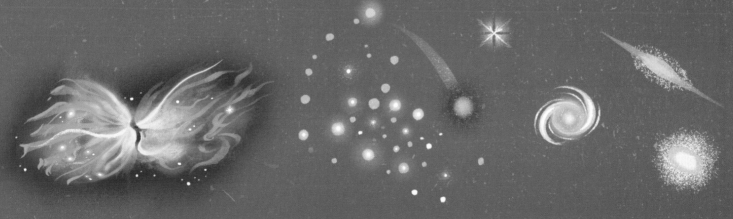

Nebulae   Stars   Galaxies

CHAPTER ONE

UNDERSTANDING THE UNIVERSE

There is nothing quite as magical and mysterious as the vast expanse of space that makes our universe.

In this chapter, we will take you on a journey from the moment the universe began, through its early stages of growing, to when it began to form atoms, then stars, planets, and galaxies. You will learn about the strangest stars—big and small—as well as the puzzling existence of black holes and the mysterious dark universe we know barely anything about.

The beginning

The universe started with what is known as "the big bang." In a single moment about 13.8 billion years ago, the first building blocks of matter burst into existence. In the beginning, the universe was extremely small and hot—it looked nothing like it does today.

1 The big bang

Nobody knows what happened before the big bang. Everything we can see in space tells us the universe started out tiny, and was packed full of energy and matter. Then, very quickly, it began to expand and cool down.

The universe is almost 14 billion years old!

How do we know the age of the universe?

Telescopes that allow us to see across vast distances in space can also allow us to see back in time. By looking at light from the oldest stars and by seeing how quickly the universe is expanding, astronomers can figure out how long ago the big bang happened.

Powerful telescopes such as NASA's James Webb Space Telescope can see clusters of distant galaxies.

Matter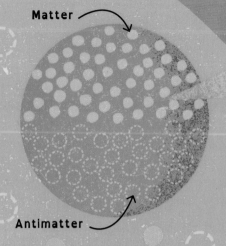

Antimatter

2 Matter and antimatter

In the big bang, two kinds of particles were produced: matter and antimatter. When matter and antimatter smash together, they get rid of each other. It means that there must have been more matter to start with.

A neutron is made of one up quark and two down quarks.

Up quark

Down quark

3 Protons and neutrons

Once the universe was cool enough, tiny particles, called "up quarks" and "down quarks," began to clump together to form slightly bigger particles, called "protons" and "neutrons." Along with electron particles, these are the building blocks of all the matter we know of today.

A proton is made of one down quark and two up quarks.

9

A growing universe

Not long after the big bang, in the universe's first moments, it began to grow bigger extremely quickly. It then went through several stages of development, changing from a mess of particles to the universe that we know today.

4 Opaque universe

In the beginning, all the particles in the universe were so hot and packed so closely together that they stopped light from moving around. The universe was "opaque," meaning it blocked light.

5 Recombination

When the universe was about 400,000 years old, it cooled down so much that particles stopped bouncing off each other. They then came together to form atoms, which are the building blocks of all matter.

Hydrogen atom

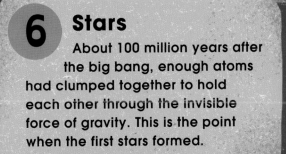

6 Stars

About 100 million years after the big bang, enough atoms had clumped together to hold each other through the invisible force of gravity. This is the point when the first stars formed.

7 Galaxies

Galaxies are collections made up of billions of stars. Astronomers think the first galaxies formed around 1 to 2 billion years after the big bang.

Looking back in time

Light takes time to reach our eyes. When we look farther into the distance, we can see further back in time.

Cosmic microwave background

When the atoms formed, light could move around the universe for the first time. We can still see this light today—it is called the cosmic microwave background.

How planets form

Before rocky planets such as Earth are born, there is just dust and gas around a star. Over a very long time, that dust and gas start to gather. The more material there is, the stronger the force of gravity, the more it sticks together. Here is how planet Earth formed.

When the chunks of rock are big enough, they form mini planets. These are called planetesimals. They make the beginnings of a planet.

1 Dusty disk
Pieces of dust start to spin and merge, getting bigger and bigger. Eventually, these tiny dust particles turn into larger rocks that together form a flat disk shape.

Big chunks of this dust, rock, and ice still exist in the solar system today and are called comets. They are also known as dirty snowballs.

Gas giants

Astronomers think that, like rocky planets, gas giants start from a disk of dust and gas around a star. Gas giants tend to develop farther away from the star, where the disk is less dense and colder. This allows gases to collapse and form a planet.

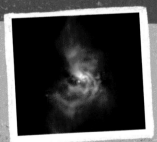

A gas giant starts as a disk of dust, called a planetary embryo.

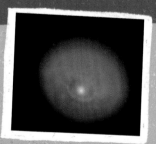

When the embryo is big enough, it starts to suck gas in from its surroundings.

Over a long time, enough gas is sucked in to make a gas giant.

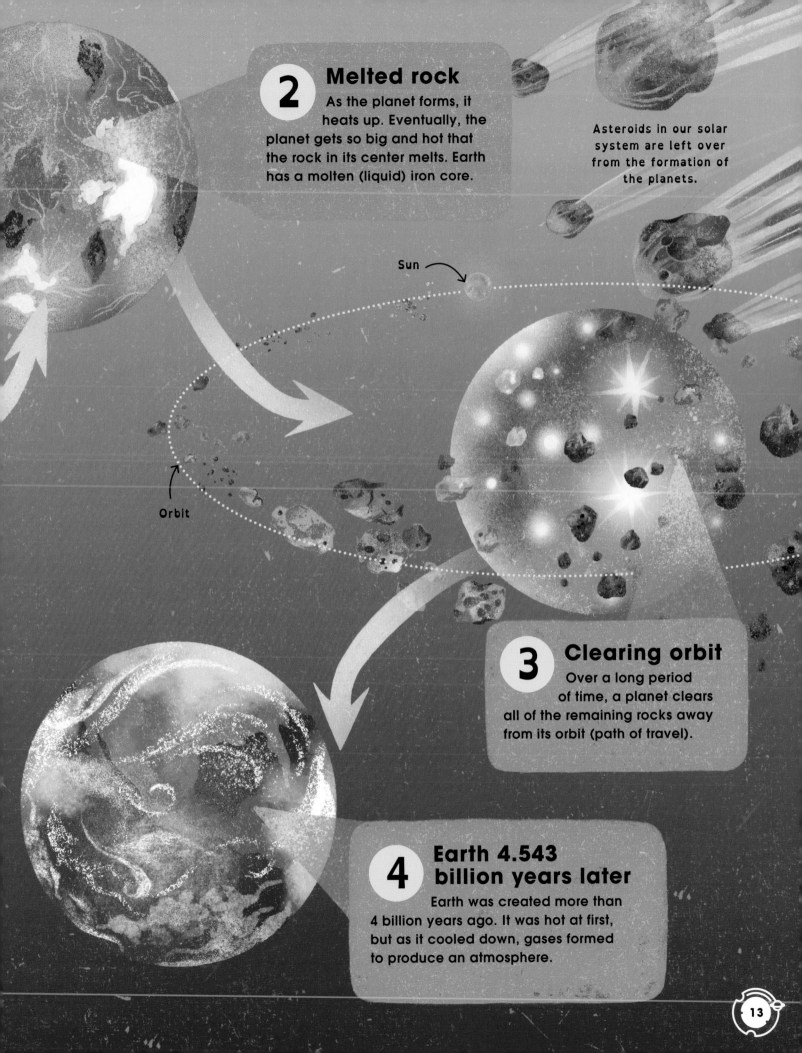

2 Melted rock

As the planet forms, it heats up. Eventually, the planet gets so big and hot that the rock in its center melts. Earth has a molten (liquid) iron core.

Asteroids in our solar system are left over from the formation of the planets.

Sun

Orbit

3 Clearing orbit

Over a long period of time, a planet clears all of the remaining rocks away from its orbit (path of travel).

4 Earth 4.543 billion years later

Earth was created more than 4 billion years ago. It was hot at first, but as it cooled down, gases formed to produce an atmosphere.

The birth of a star

Stars, like the sun, are massive spheres (balls) of gas. At the core of every star is a reaction called nuclear fusion. This keeps the star burning and releasing light. Yet stars start their lives as something much more boring that does not glow at all.

1 Nebula

A huge cloud of dust and gas in space is called a nebula. When a nebula gets big enough, the cloud starts to pull together because of a force called gravity.

2 Collapse!

Eventually, after shrinking for long enough, parts of the nebula will collapse into a clump. The material in the clump is squeezed so tightly together that it starts to warm up.

3 Protostars

When a clump first forms, it spends a while as something called a protostar. At this stage, it is still surrounded by a cloud of dust. It is not yet hot enough to be a star.

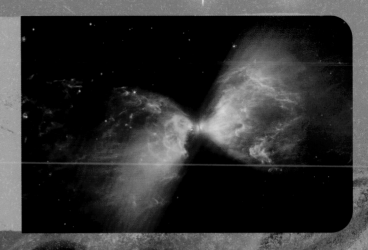

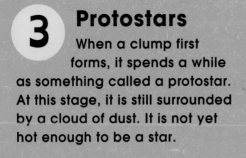

4 Stars forming

When the clump has dragged in enough material, a process known as nuclear fusion happens in the middle. A huge amount of energy is released, which blows the dust around the clump away to reveal a star.

Star power

Everything in the universe is made up of tiny particles, called atoms. When certain atoms collide with enough energy, they combine to form new atoms. A huge amount of energy is also released, along with smaller particles, called neutrons. This reaction keeps stars burning.

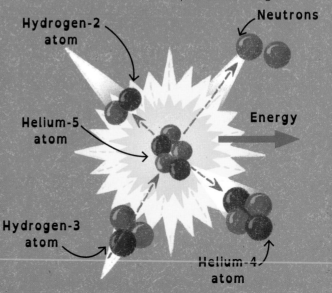

Hydrogen-2 atom

Neutrons

Helium-5 atom

Energy

Hydrogen-3 atom

Helium-4 atom

Types of stars

Stars come in all types of sizes and colors. We group them depending on how big they are and what color light they shine. Red and orange stars are the coolest, while white and blue stars are the hottest. In the middle are yellow stars.

When stars like the sun run out of fuel, they swell and become much brighter. This is a red giant. Our sun will be a red giant in about 5 billion years.

White dwarfs

A white dwarf is about one-hundredth of the radius (the distance from the center to the surface) of our sun. But it has about the same mass.

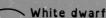
White dwarf

The surface of the sun is about 9,900°F (5,500°C). Its core (center) is much hotter.

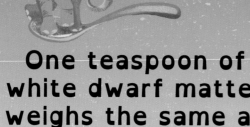

One teaspoon of white dwarf matter weighs the same as a 6-ton elephant on Earth!

Sunlike stars

Most stars are part of a group astronomers call the main sequence. These medium-sized stars can live for about 10 billion years.

Giants

Giant stars can be anything from 10 to 100 times the radius of the sun, but with up to eight times the mass.

Cassiopeia A is the remnant (remains) of a supernova in the constellation Cassiopeia.

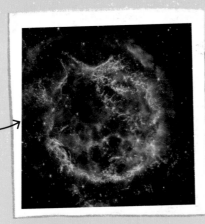

Supernova

A supernova occurs when a huge star runs out of its fuel. The star then collapses, and energy builds up to create a gigantic explosion.

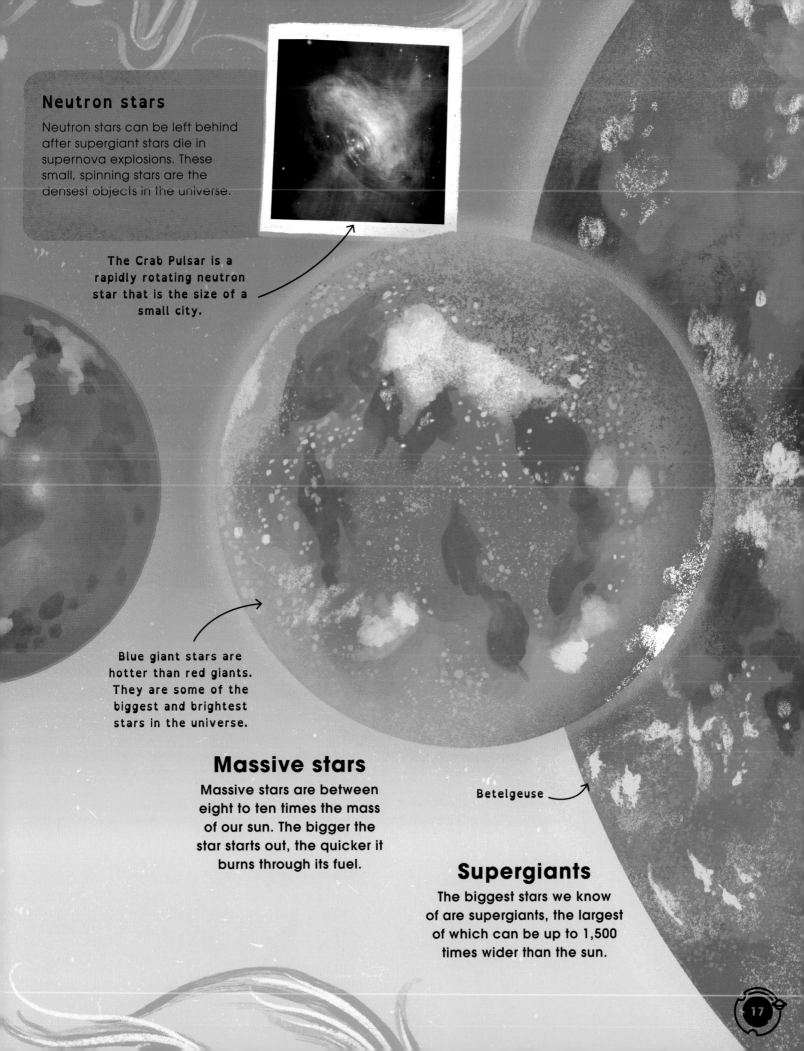

Neutron stars

Neutron stars can be left behind after supergiant stars die in supernova explosions. These small, spinning stars are the densest objects in the universe.

The Crab Pulsar is a rapidly rotating neutron star that is the size of a small city.

Blue giant stars are hotter than red giants. They are some of the biggest and brightest stars in the universe.

Massive stars

Massive stars are between eight to ten times the mass of our sun. The bigger the star starts out, the quicker it burns through its fuel.

Betelgeuse

Supergiants

The biggest stars we know of are supergiants, the largest of which can be up to 1,500 times wider than the sun.

Star clusters

Stars can exist on their own or in groups of many stars. When a group appears in the same part of the galaxy, it is called a star cluster. Sometimes, star clusters are made up of young stars that have just been born. At other times, they are clusters of dying, old stars.

Open clusters

When young stars have emerged from the same nebula (dust cloud), they are in a star cluster. Open star clusters can contain millions of stars. They remain together because they pull on each other with gravity.

The Pleiades, or the Seven Sisters, is home to more than 3,000 stars. A few of its brightest stars can be seen at night, without binoculars.

The Beehive cluster is one of the closest star clusters to Earth. It is home to about 1,000 stars.

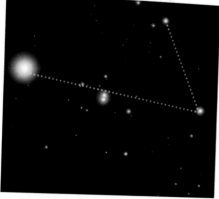

The Hyades cluster is a group of hundreds of stars that make a V-shape in the night sky.

Holding it together

Gravity is a force that acts between all objects with a mass. We are able to live on Earth because gravity attracts us and Earth to each other. The farther one object is from another, the weaker gravity gets. In star clusters, the stars are close enough for gravity to keep them together.

Gravity pulls stars together.

Globular clusters

Ancient stars group together into what is known as a globular cluster. The Omega Centauri globular cluster is made of 10 million stars, visible with the naked eye from the Southern Hemisphere.

Omega Centauri is one of the biggest globular clusters in our galaxy.

Embedded clusters

Some open clusters remain surrounded by the cloud that they were made from. These are called embedded clusters. The Orion nebula is an embedded cluster.

Nebulae

We know that stars begin life as a cloud of dust called a nebula, of which there are many different types. Stars leave nebulae behind when they die, in dramatic explosions. The massive layers of dust and gases that remain after these blasts can look beautiful.

Many nebulae shine because of energy coming from the gases they contain. Different gases can emit light in many colors.

Diffuse nebulae

A nebula is called diffuse when it does not have a clear edge. This applies to most of the nebulae we can see from Earth. In small telescopes, they look like faint blobs.

Some nebulae, such as the Witch Head Nebula, do not emit their own light. They reflect light from nearby stars, like cats' eyes glowing with reflected light in the dark.

Supernova remnants

When the biggest stars die, they create a huge explosion. This is called a supernova. After the explosion, a supernova leaves behind a nebula.

The Crab Nebula was discovered in 1843, but Chinese astronomers saw the supernova from Earth in 1054.

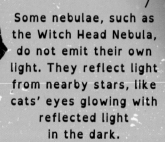

Planetary nebulae

A planetary nebula has nothing to do with planets. It is the name for what we see when a star dies. The star gets rid of its outer layers, and this is what creates the nebula. Early astronomers thought that these looked like planets.

The Ring Nebula was one of the first planetary nebulae to be discovered. It was spotted by an astronomer named Charles Messier in 1779, while he was looking for comets.

Stellar nurseries

The types of nebulae in which stars are born are known as stellar nurseries. Stars that form from the same nebula turn into groups of stars called open star clusters.

The clouds in the Eagle Nebula are known as the "Pillars of Creation."

The death of a star

Stars can die in dramatic ways, but what each death looks like depends on how big the star is. The smallest stars die by collapsing, while medium-sized stars expand and then collapse. The biggest stars end their lives in dramatic explosions. The very largest stars leave behind black holes.

Sunlike star

The hydrogen that fuels stars such as the sun lasts for 10 billion years. Then the hydrogen in their core runs out.

Red giant

When all the hydrogen is used up, a star starts to burn helium in its shell. It then swells up and becomes what is known as a red giant.

Massive star

Large stars burn through their hydrogen quickly. For some, this could be as little as 20 million years, which is a short amount of time for a star.

Red supergiant

After the biggest stars run out of hydrogen, they turn into red supergiants. These are the largest stars in the universe.

Planetary nebula

When all of its fuel has run out, a star gets rid of its outer layers. These turn into a cloud around the star called a planetary nebula.

White dwarf

After the cloud and dust around the star float away, a type of star called a white dwarf is left behind. A white dwarf can be as hot as 180,000°F (100,000°C).

Black dwarf

A black dwarf is thought to be the result of a white dwarf totally cooling down over hundreds of billions of years.

Neutron star

Of the stars that go supernova, the smaller ones leave an incredibly dense neutron star behind.

Supernova

When supergiants use up all their fuel, they collapse and create a spectacular explosion called a supernova. These can be seen across the universe.

Black hole

The biggest supernovae leave behind black holes. These regions of space are so dense that nothing can escape—not even light.

Galaxies

A huge collections of stars bound together by gravity is called a galaxy. There are billions of galaxies spread throughout the universe, ranging from dwarf galaxies with only a few billion stars, to giant galaxies that span millions of light years across. We live in the Milky Way galaxy, which is home to hundreds of billions of stars.

Spiral galaxies

This type of galaxy is shaped a bit like a fried egg, with a central bulge surrounded by a flat disk made up of spiraling arms. In many spiral galaxies, the arms sweep out from the middle of the central bulge. About 60 percent of all galaxies are spiral galaxies, including our own Milky Way. Astronomers think that most spiral galaxies eventually turn into elliptical galaxies.

M74 is a spiral-shaped galaxy, with two main arms.

Spiral arms

Extremely hot, young stars glow blue in the arms of the Pinwheel galaxy.

Barred spiral galaxy

When a spiral galaxy's arms do not start in the galaxy's very center, but instead from a central line of stars, this is called a barred spiral galaxy. The Pinwheel galaxy is a barred spiral galaxy that is much bigger than the Milky Way.

Spiral galaxy

Messier 74, also known as the Phantom galaxy, is a spiral galaxy about 32 million light years from our solar system. It faces us directly, so we can clearly see its two spiral arms.

Galaxy clusters

Galaxies group together to form clumps called galaxy clusters. The Milky Way is part of a cluster known as the Local Group, containing 80 galaxies. The Local Group is then part of an even bigger structure called a supercluster, which contains 100 galaxy clusters. There are thought to be millions of superclusters in the universe.

This galaxy cluster is called Abell 1689.

Elliptical galaxies

After spiral galaxies, the most common galaxy shape is elliptical. These galaxies often have an overall oval shape, but they come in a bigger range of sizes than any other type of galaxy. The smallest and largest galaxies ever discovered are both elliptical.

Most elliptical galaxies are full of old, dying stars—but NGC 2865 contains many young stars.

NGC 2865 is a rapidly rotating elliptical galaxy.

The stars in a galaxy move around a central point.

Lenticular galaxies

Lenticular galaxies are disk shaped. They have a central bulge, similar to spiral and elliptical galaxies, but no spiral arms.

There are up to 200 billion galaxies in the universe.

The lenticular galaxy NGC 4452 can look flat in pictures, but it is actually a thin disk.

Irregular galaxies

Galaxies with no particular shape are known as irregular galaxies. Most of these are smaller dwarf galaxies, with only a few billion stars.

NGC 7292's center is stretched out into a distinct bar, a feature usually seen in spiral galaxies.

NGC 7292 is an irregular galaxy.

Where are we?

It is almost impossible to imagine just how big our universe is, but we can try. We live on a planet that orbits a star. Our star, the sun, is one of billions of stars in the Milky Way, which itself is just one of billions of galaxies in the universe.

Arc of the Milky Way

Local Group

Our galaxy is part of a group of galaxies known as the Local Group. The biggest galaxy in this group is called Andromeda. In about four billion years, the Milky Way will collide with Andromeda.

Milky Way galaxy

The Milky Way is a galaxy that contains billions of stars like our sun. In the middle of the galaxy sits an object as heavy as four million suns, called a supermassive black hole.

Andromeda

Milky Way

Triangulum galaxy

Planet Earth is here

Virgo supercluster

Galaxy clusters contain many more galaxies than galaxy groups, and superclusters are collections of both. The Virgo supercluster contains about 100 galaxy clusters, including the Local Group. Superclusters bunch together to make the biggest structures in the universe.

Local Group

This pair of galaxies are known as The Eyes.

Telescopes such as the James Webb Space Telescope can see the Virgo supercluster by looking at all the galaxies near us in the universe.

Cosmic web

Galaxy superclusters link together throughout the universe in a shape a bit like a spider's web. This huge structure is called the cosmic web.

Filaments

Voids

Since the universe has no real edge, scientists find it hard to tell what shape it is.

Black holes

Black holes are created by collapsing stars, and are the strangest things in the universe. They are areas of space where gravity is so strong that, beyond a point, nothing can escape. We have seen black holes thanks to the large amounts of energy that they create. There are even photographs of two of them.

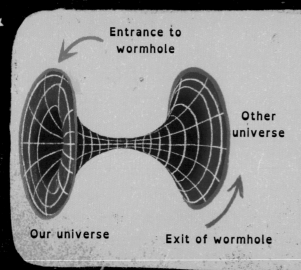

Entrance to wormhole

Other universe

Our universe

Exit of wormhole

Wormhole

A tunnel between two black holes is called a wormhole. We have never seen evidence of wormholes, but they are predicted by some theories. If they exist, something could enter a wormhole in one universe and emerge in another.

Spaghettification

When something approaches a black hole, the gravity on the front of it is so strong that it gets stretched into a long strand. The name given to this effect is spaghettification.

Stellar black hole

Stellar black holes are the mass left behind when the biggest stars die. They release powerful jets of high-energy particles and radiation from the center of the hole, which is called the accretion disk.

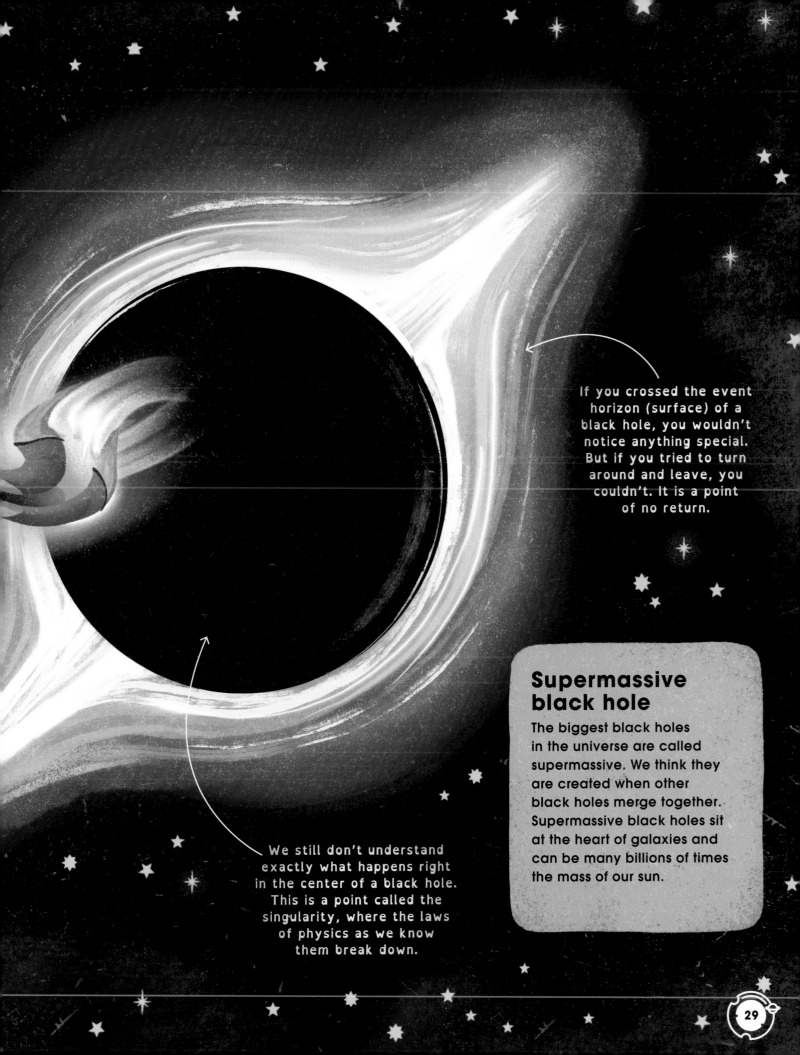

If you crossed the event horizon (surface) of a black hole, you wouldn't notice anything special. But if you tried to turn around and leave, you couldn't. It is a point of no return.

Supermassive black hole

The biggest black holes in the universe are called supermassive. We think they are created when other black holes merge together. Supermassive black holes sit at the heart of galaxies and can be many billions of times the mass of our sun.

We still don't understand exactly what happens right in the center of a black hole. This is a point called the singularity, where the laws of physics as we know them break down.

The dark universe

We know a lot about the universe, but there is still a huge amount we do not understand. In fact, most of the energy in the universe is hidden in things we cannot see or explain. For this reason, we call it the dark universe.

We can see stars and galaxies because of the light they emit or reflect. The type of material that interacts with light is called matter.

What is the universe made of?

The stuff we are made of, normal matter, only makes up a tiny fraction of the universe. The rest is dark matter—which we can detect through its gravity—and a mysterious force called dark energy.

5%
matter

27%
dark matter

We cannot see dark matter, but we know that it is there. We can see the effect it has on stars and galaxies around it through gravity.

68%
dark energy

The universe is getting bigger, and the rate it is expanding is getting faster. We don't know what is forcing it apart, so we call it dark energy.

The future of the universe

The fate of the universe depends on how much dark matter and dark energy there is in it. Dark matter keeps the universe together through gravity, but dark energy forces it apart.

If there is too much dark energy, the universe will continue to speed up in its expansion, and could rip itself apart.

If there is too much dark matter, the universe will stop expanding and eventually collapse.

If there is just the right balance of dark matter and dark energy, the universe will continue expanding, and it will eventually get cold and dark.

Dark matter

All we know about dark matter is that it is affected by gravity. We don't know if there is a dark matter equivalent of every normal matter particle, or if it looks totally different.

Dark matter could be huge objects in space, called massive astrophysical compact halo objects (MACHOs). We have not found any of these yet.

MACHO

Luminous matter

Dark matter

Another view is that dark matter is made of particles. A group of particles called weakly interacting massive particles (WIMPs) might explain dark matter.

CHAPTER TWO

THE SOLAR SYSTEM AND BEYOND

Our little part of the Milky Way might be closer to home than distant galaxies, but there are still plenty of mysteries left about the solar system.

From our dazzling sun that provides us with energy and light, to the coldest depths of the icy outer reaches of the Kuiper Belt, in this section we will explore everything we know about our solar system. We will visit exciting moons and planets with wild weather, as well as look beyond our home to planets that orbit other stars, called exoplanets.

The sun

The sun is the star at the center of our solar system. It came into existence about 4.5 billion years ago. Like all stars, the sun is fueled by a powerful process called nuclear fusion—which creates huge amounts of energy. This energy gives us the light and heat that we need to survive.

Photosphere

Solar flare

Sun spot

Solar prominence

Layers of the sun

The sun is made up of various layers. A hot, dense core sits at its center. This is where nuclear fusion takes place, creating the sun's energy. The next layer out is the radiative zone, which is followed by the convection zone. The mysterious outermost layer is the corona.

Core
The core is the hottest part of the sun, with a temperature of 18,000,000°F (15,000,000°C).

Radiative zone
Here the temperature is about 14,400,000°F (8,000,000°C). Light moves through it to the surface.

Convection zone
The temperature here is around 900,000°F (500,000°C). Light in this layer eventually escapes.

What is the sun made of?

The sun is a giant ball of electrically charged atoms, called plasma. Three quarters of the atoms are hydrogen, and just under a quarter are helium. A tiny fraction of the atoms are made up of 65 other elements, including oxygen, carbon, and nitrogen.

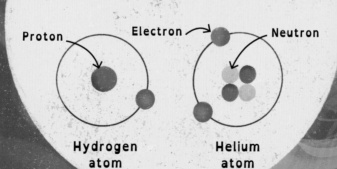

Proton   Electron   Neutron

Hydrogen atom   Helium atom

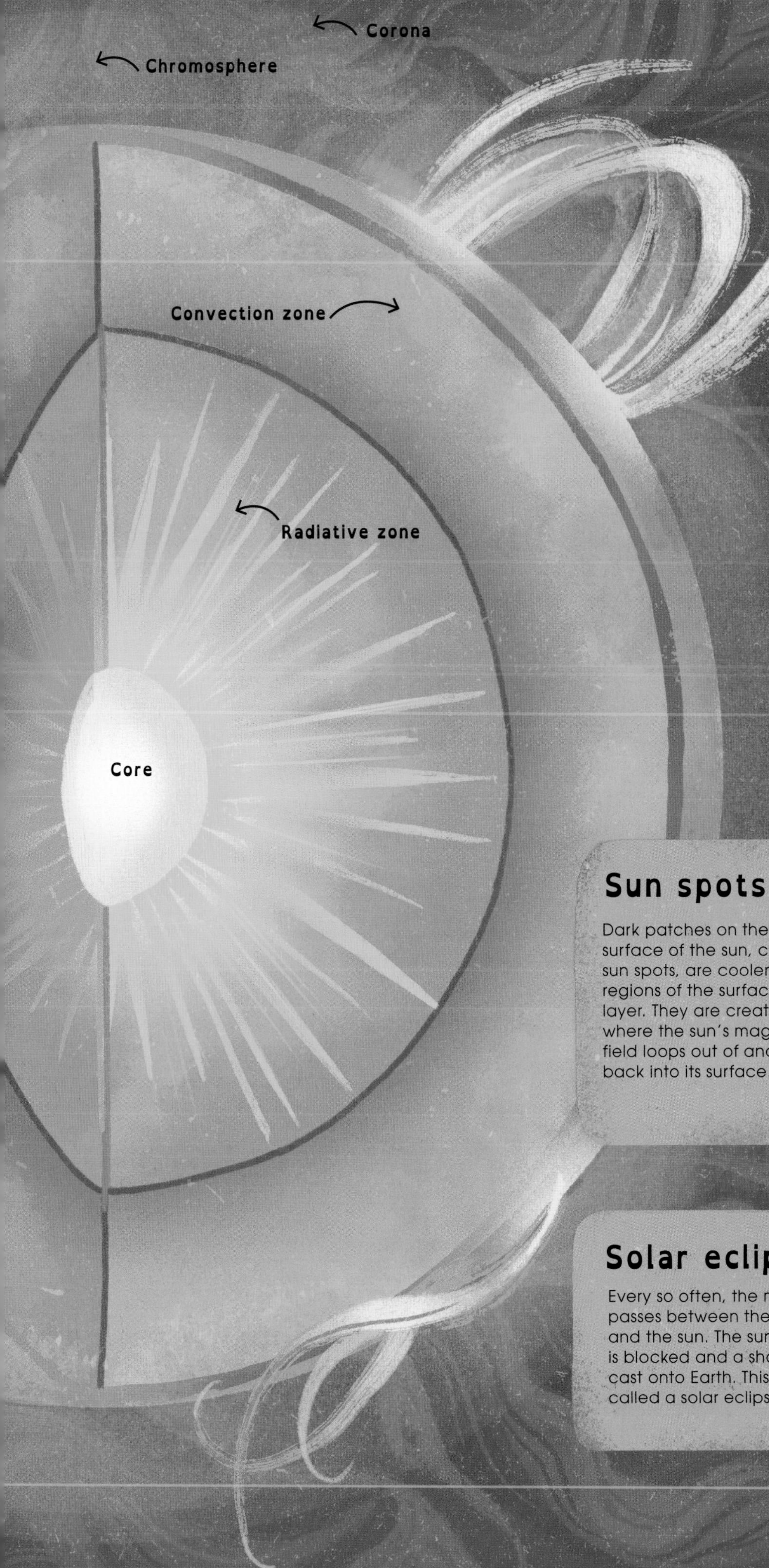

Corona

Chromosphere

Convection zone

Radiative zone

Core

Size of the sun

The sun is 870,000 miles (1.4 million kilometers) wide—about one million Earths could fit inside it! The sun makes up 99.8 percent of the entire mass of the solar system.

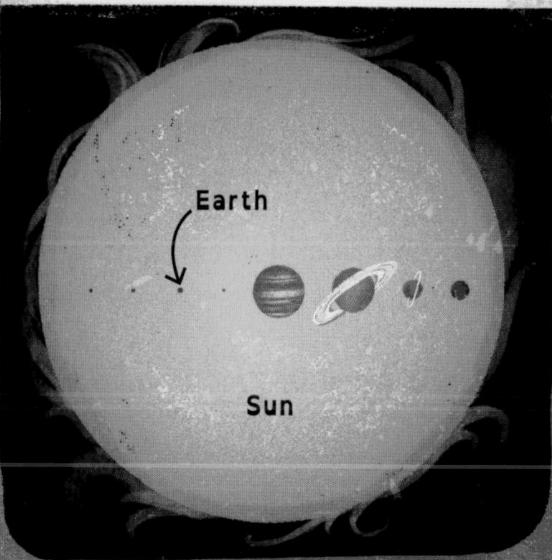

Earth

Sun

Sun spots

Dark patches on the surface of the sun, called sun spots, are cooler regions of the surface layer. They are created where the sun's magnetic field loops out of and back into its surface.

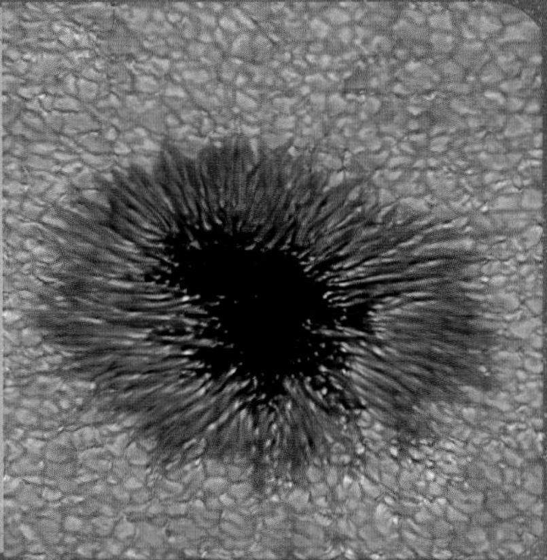

Solar eclipse

Every so often, the moon passes between the Earth and the sun. The sun's light is blocked and a shadow is cast onto Earth. This is called a solar eclipse.

The moon

The moon is Earth's only natural satellite. It is our closest celestial body—and the only one that we have stepped foot on. The moon was created within the first 100,000 years of Earth's life, about 4.5 billion years ago. The lighter parts on the surface are the moon's highlands, and the darker parts are plains, or "seas," of hardened lava from ancient volcanic eruptions.

Plato

Copernicus

Aristarchus

Kepler

Craters on the moon

The moon is covered in craters formed from comets and asteroids crashing into its surface over billions of years. The volcanoes that once spewed lava across its surface are no longer active, so the craters stay visible.

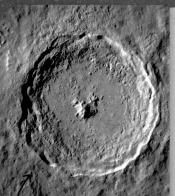

The Tycho crater is about 108 million years old.

Moon phases

The moon completes an orbit of Earth every 29.5 days. As it moves around us, different parts of it reflect the sun's light back at us, so we see different shapes at different phases. When the moon appears to grow, it is "waxing," when it seems to shrink, it is "waning."

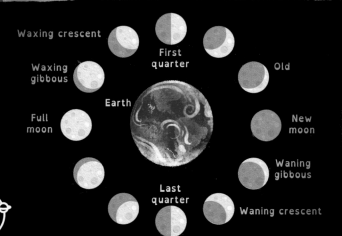

Waxing crescent

Waxing gibbous

First quarter

Old

Earth

Full moon

New moon

Last quarter

Waning gibbous

Waning crescent

Sun

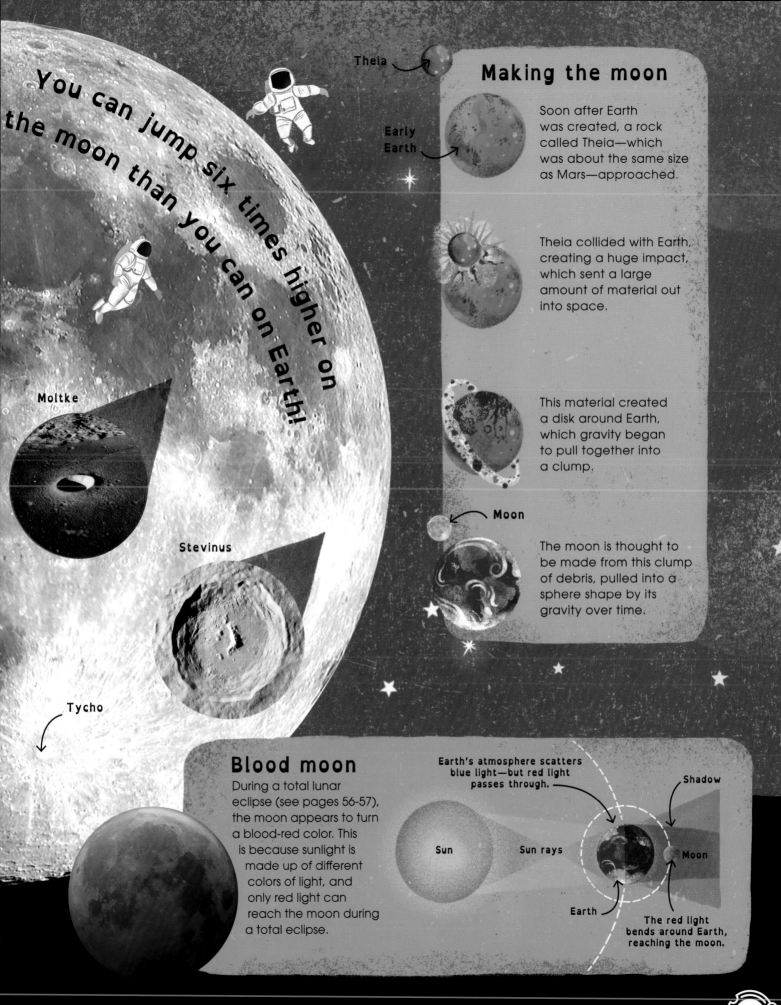

You can jump six times higher on the moon than you can on Earth!

Moltke

Stevinus

Tycho

Making the moon

Theia

Early Earth

Soon after Earth was created, a rock called Theia—which was about the same size as Mars—approached.

Theia collided with Earth, creating a huge impact, which sent a large amount of material out into space.

This material created a disk around Earth, which gravity began to pull together into a clump.

Moon

The moon is thought to be made from this clump of debris, pulled into a sphere shape by its gravity over time.

Blood moon

During a total lunar eclipse (see pages 56-57), the moon appears to turn a blood-red color. This is because sunlight is made up of different colors of light, and only red light can reach the moon during a total eclipse.

Earth's atmosphere scatters blue light—but red light passes through.

Shadow

Sun

Sun rays

Moon

Earth

The red light bends around Earth, reaching the moon.

The solar system

Earth belongs to a family of planets called the solar system, which was born about 4.5 billion years ago. The sun is at the center of the solar system, and the planets spill out in a disk shape around it. Our solar system is just one of many planetary systems in the universe—we know of more than 3,200 other stars with planets orbiting them, and there could be many more out there...

Eight planets

There are eight planets in the solar system, orbiting the sun. The four closest to the sun are rocky planets, such as Earth. The four farthest away from the sun are much bigger, with no solid surface.

Earth

Mars

The asteroid belt between Mars and Jupiter

Uranus

Jupiter

How long is a year?

The length of a year is different on each planet, depending on how long it takes to complete one orbit of the sun. On Earth, a year is 365 days, but a year on Jupiter is about 4,333 Earth days.

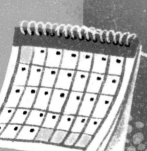

Neptune

The Goldilocks zone

There is a region around every star called the Goldilocks zone, where it is just the right temperature for liquid water to exist on a planet's surface. Too close and it would be too hot, too far away and it's too cold.

It would take 20 years for humans to reach Neptune!

Sun

Venus

Mercury

Planet orbits

Goldilocks zone

Saturn

The Kuiper Belt beyond Neptune

How big is it?

The size of the solar system can be measured by how long light takes to travel through it. It takes light from the sun 8 minutes to reach Earth, but 4 hours to travel to the planet Neptune.

The rocky planets

The four closest planets to the sun are great balls of rock with solid surfaces, called the rocky planets. They vary in size and temperature, with Mercury being the smallest and Venus the hottest. Earth is the third planet from the sun.

Mercury

Mercury is the smallest and closest planet to the sun. It is just over a third of the Earth's size and orbits the sun in 88 days. Its surface is covered in craters and mountains.

Venus

Slightly smaller than Earth, Venus is a fiery world covered in ancient volcanoes. It has a thick atmosphere with an extremely hot climate.

Ceres

The dwarf planet Ceres is located in part of the solar system called the asteroid belt, which is home to large rocks left over from the formation of the solar system. Ceres is the biggest asteroid of them all, as well as being classified as a dwarf planet.

Bright spots on the surface show where mini meteorites have hit.

Ceres is the largest object in the asteroid belt between Mars and Jupiter, and the closest dwarf planet to Earth.

Earth

Earth is the only planet in the solar system known to be home to any life. It is called the blue planet because its surface is mostly made up of oceans.

Olympus Mons 16 miles (25 km)

Mount Everest 29,032 ft (8,849 m)

Olympus Mons is the tallest mountain in the solar system. This ancient volcano on Mars is three times the height of Mount Everest, Earth's highest mountain.

Earth's atmosphere can be seen here as a thin blue line.

Mars

Mars is known as the red planet, and is our closest neighboring planet. Its surface is dotted with mountain ranges, ancient volcanoes, and deep channels. This leads astronomers to believe that Mars was covered with deep oceans billions of years ago.

The frost line

Separating the asteroid belt from Jupiter is an imaginary line, called the frost line. Beyond this line, it is so cold that water and other compounds exist in the form of solid ice rather than liquid.

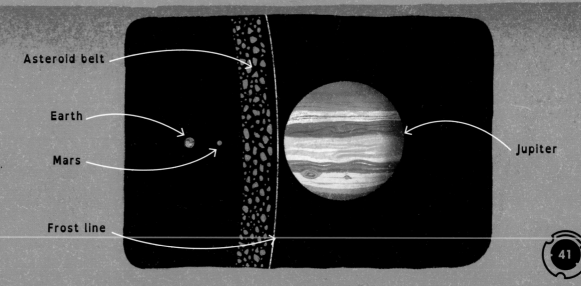

Asteroid belt

Earth

Mars

Frost line

Jupiter

The giants

The fifth and sixth planets from the sun are called the gas giants, because they do not have a solid surface, but are made of gas. They are huge in size. The biggest of the two, Jupiter, is so large that all the other planets in the solar system could fit inside it! The two farthest planets from the sun are the ice giants, made up of gas and water.

Auroras

When particles from the sun hit Jupiter's magnetic field, they create a bright display of light called an aurora. Earth has auroras, too, called the northern and southern lights. They shine a different color from Jupiter's auroras.

Jupiter

The biggest planet in the solar system is Jupiter, which is the fifth planet from the sun. The atmosphere on this planet is constantly churning with storms—the biggest of which is its Great Red Spot—and powerful lightning.

Saturn

Saturn is the second-biggest planet in the solar system and the sixth planet from the sun. It is best known for its large ring, but it is not the only planet with rings—all of the gas giants have their own rings.

Uranus

The seventh planet from the sun spins on its side, in the opposite direction from Earth and most of the other planets. An Earth-sized object is thought to have hit Uranus at some point in the past, knocking it sideways and reversing its spin.

The ice giants Uranus and Neptune are extremely far from the sun, which means they receive very little sunlight and are VERY cold.

Icy moons

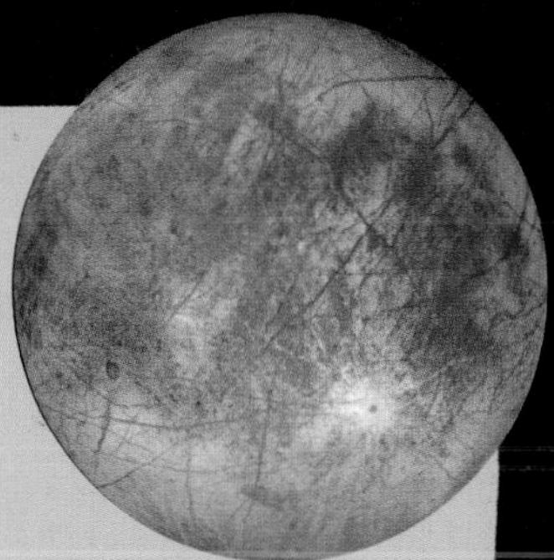

Jupiter has almost 100 known moons and Saturn has more than 140, but we keep finding new ones! Jupiter's biggest moon, Europa, is a volcanic world, while Saturn's largest moon, Enceladus, sends plumes of water vapor into space.

Europa

Enceladus

Neptune

The farthest planet from the sun is an ice giant with a stormy surface and extremely strong winds. It is surrounded by 5 recognized rings and 14 moons.

Wild planetary weather

Earth is not the only planet with clouds, rain, wind, storms, and oceans. In fact, the weather on other planets and moons can be much more dramatic than on Earth. This is because of their different sizes, as well as the range of temperatures and elements found in their atmospheres.

Clear Mars sky • Dust storm

Lightning storm

Dust devils on Mars

The surface of Mars is like a desert. Strong winds can sweep across the planet, creating whirlwinds called dust devils that drag dust around the surface. Dust devils also occur on Earth, but they are larger and more powerful on Mars.

Lightning on Jupiter

Lightning often strikes in Jupiter's stormy atmosphere—and it is much more dramatic than the type of lightning we see on Earth. Jupiter's lightning can sometimes appear neon green, because of ammonia gas in the planet's clouds.

Methane lakes on Titan

Saturn's moon, Titan, is the only body in the solar system known to have a weather cycle, like the weather cycle on Earth. The difference is that on Titan, it is too cold for water to be liquid at the surface. Instead, the lakes and clouds on Titan are made of methane gas.

Saturn

Iron rain on WASP-76b

One side of the exoplanet called WASP-76b is always facing its star. Iron on this hot, day-lit side evaporates (turns into vapor) and travels to its cooler, dark, night-locked side, where it rains down on the surface.

Space rocks

The solar system is filled with pieces of rock and metal left over from when the planets formed. Space rocks mostly fit into two categories—asteroids or comets. Sometimes, bits of asteroids or comets hit Earth, but most space rocks can only be viewed with telescopes, far off in the distance.

Meteor showers

When Earth moves through a patch of debris left behind by an asteroid or comet, there are many more meteors in the sky. This is called a meteor shower.

Meteors

Meteors, or shooting stars, are flashes of light in the night sky. They appear when a piece of dust or rock from space enters Earth's atmosphere and burns up.

Meteorites

Most space rocks that hit Earth burn up in the atmosphere. But if they are large enough, part of them can survive the journey and fall to the ground, becoming a meteorite.

The Hoba meteorite in Namibia is the largest known one on Earth.

Asteroids

Asteroids are lumps of rock and metal that orbit the sun. Most of them can be found between Mars and Jupiter in the main asteroid belt, but some also orbit closer to Earth.

Most comets appear to be blue. The green comet's color is because it is made up of carbon and nitrogen.

Comets

Comets are rocky, icy snowballs that orbit the sun much farther away than asteroids. They start beyond the orbit of Neptune.

Types of rock

Most of the meteorites found on Earth are stony. A small amount are made of iron-nickel alloys (mixtures of different metals) and just over one percent are half stone and half metal.

Stone meteorite

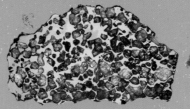

Iron and stone meteorite

Iron-rich meteorite

Beyond Neptune

The most distant part of our solar system is a cold, dark, and mysterious place. Beyond the orbit of Neptune, about 2.8 billion miles (4.5 billion km) from the sun, is an icy disk full of rocks called the Kuiper Belt. This is where you will find Pluto.

Pluto

Once thought to be a planet, Pluto is now classified as a dwarf planet. It is an icy world with mountains and volcanoes, orbited by five moons. At 620 miles (1,000 km) across, it is the largest known dwarf planet.

Pluto

Dwarf planets

Planets are so big that their gravity pulls in nearby objects, clearing their orbits—dwarf planets are big, but not big enough to do this. There are five known dwarf planets in the solar system, one in the asteroid belt, and four in the Kuiper Belt.

Ceres is the only dwarf planet in the asteroid belt. It is both an asteroid and a dwarf planet.

Eris is just a little smaller than Pluto, but it has more mass and only one moon.

Makemake takes 305 Earth years to orbit the sun. It is just under two-thirds the size of Pluto.

Haumea is the shape of an egg and has rings around it, as well as two moons.

The Kuiper Belt

The doughnut-shaped disk of rocky objects beyond Neptune is called the Kuiper Belt. It is thought to be home to millions of objects, but since it is too far away to easily study, only 2,000 have been discovered.

The Kuiper Belt

The Oort Cloud

The Oort cloud

Astronomers have never seen the Oort cloud. They believe it is an icy sphere covering the entire solar system, beyond the Kuiper Belt. Some comets that we see in our night sky are thought to come from there.

Solar system

Voyager 1

The *Voyager 1* spacecraft left Earth in 1977, just two weeks after *Voyager 2*. The two have been traveling deeper into space ever since then. They left the solar system in 2012 and still send signals back to Earth every day.

Planet 9

Some astronomers think there could be another planet in our solar system, beyond the orbit of Neptune, known as Planet 9. This is because some Kuiper Belt objects seem to move as though there is a planet nearby. This mysterious body, however, has never been seen.

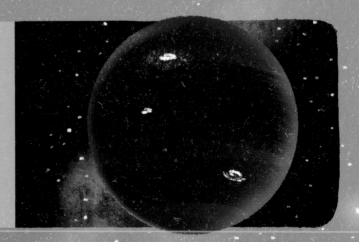

Exoplanets

Astronomers think that most stars, like our sun, have planets orbiting them. Planets that orbit other stars are called exoplanets, and we have discovered more than 5,500 of them so far. The main types of exoplanet are: Neptunian, gas giants, super-Earths, and terrestrial.

Kepler-421b

51 Pegasi b

Gas giants

Astronomers have found about 1,800 gas giant exoplanets. Just like Jupiter and Saturn in our solar system, gas giants are large planets without rocky surfaces. They are mostly made of the gases hydrogen and helium. Gas giant exoplanets have been found orbiting much closer to their stars than Jupiter or Saturn to our sun.

Neptunian

These exoplanets are about the same size as Neptune or Uranus, which means they are about four times the size of Earth. Like Neptune and Uranus, their atmospheres contain the gases hydrogen and helium, but their cores are made of rock and metals. We have found almost 2,000 Neptunian exoplanets. Mini-Neptune exoplanets are bigger than Earth but smaller than Neptune.

Finding exoplanets

Most exoplanets cannot be seen directly, so astronomers have found clever ways to discover them.

Transit method

Sensitive telescopes are used to study the brightness of distant stars. If a star's brightness dims, an exoplanet may be passing in front of it.

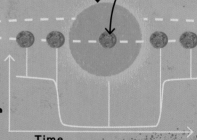

Star   Exoplanet

Brightness

Time

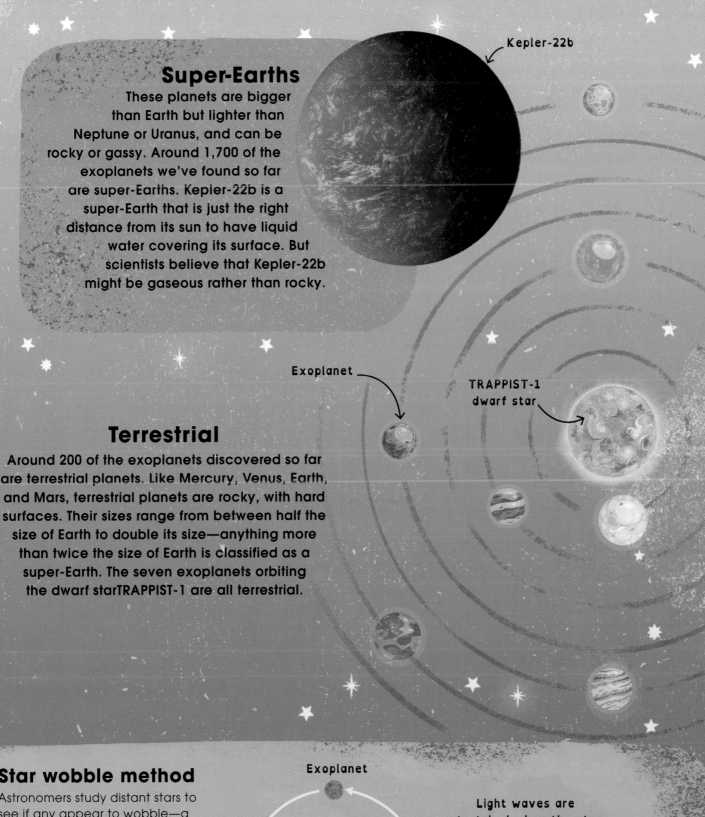

Super-Earths

These planets are bigger than Earth but lighter than Neptune or Uranus, and can be rocky or gassy. Around 1,700 of the exoplanets we've found so far are super-Earths. Kepler-22b is a super-Earth that is just the right distance from its sun to have liquid water covering its surface. But scientists believe that Kepler-22b might be gaseous rather than rocky.

Kepler-22b

Exoplanet

TRAPPIST-1 dwarf star

Terrestrial

Around 200 of the exoplanets discovered so far are terrestrial planets. Like Mercury, Venus, Earth, and Mars, terrestrial planets are rocky, with hard surfaces. Their sizes range from between half the size of Earth to double its size—anything more than twice the size of Earth is classified as a super-Earth. The seven exoplanets orbiting the dwarf starTRAPPIST-1 are all terrestrial.

Star wobble method

Astronomers study distant stars to see if any appear to wobble—a wobbly star suggests an exoplanet is present. As an exoplanet moves around a star, its gravity pulls on the star—causing the star to wobble. Astronomers detect wobbles from Earth by studying changes in the light waves that come from stars.

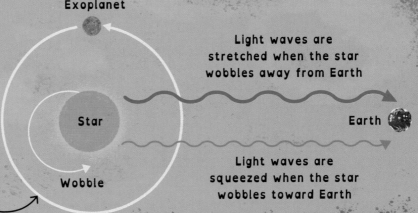

Exoplanet

Light waves are stretched when the star wobbles away from Earth

Star

Earth

Wobble

Light waves are squeezed when the star wobbles toward Earth

Exoplanet's orbit

CHAPTER THREE

THE UNIVERSE AND US

Humans have looked up at the stars for thousands of years, full of wonder. Now, thanks to technology, we are able to explore space like never before.

Navigating the night sky using just their eyes, ancient peoples were able to spot patterns of bright stars and name them. This chapter will teach you the names of some of these patterns, as well as other features to help you find your way around the night sky by sight. Here, you can also meet some of the brave people who have been into space, and learn how you might one day become one of them.

Looking at space

We are only able to see a few thousand stars with our eyes. To see more distant stars, galaxies, and nebulae, we have to use telescopes. Some telescopes are built on the ground, while others are sent up into space for a closer look. As telescope technology improves, we can see ever-clearer images of things farther and farther away.

Seeing the invisible

Light travels in waves with different wavelengths—some of which we can't see. Infrared light from stars is invisible to our eyes, but special telescopes can pick it up. Other telescopes can pick up invisible waves of radiation, such as X-rays, from space objects.

Radio waves · Infrared · X-ray

Visible wavelength

Wavelength

FAST

The Five-hundred-meter Aperture Spherical radio Telescope (FAST) is the world's largest telescope. It became fully operational in 2020, and picks up radio waves released by objects in space. It discovered the largest gas cloud ever recorded— a hydrogen cloud 20 times bigger than the Milky Way.

Measuring 1,640 ft (500 m) across, FAST covers a huge area of land in southwest China.

ELT

The Extremely Large Telescope (ELT) is now being built in Chile's Atacama Desert. When it is completed in 2028, it will be the world's biggest telescope that sees visible and infrared light, using a huge mirror measuring 128 ft (39 m).

The ELT is being built on a mountain called Cerro Armazones, which is 9,993 ft (3,046 m) high.

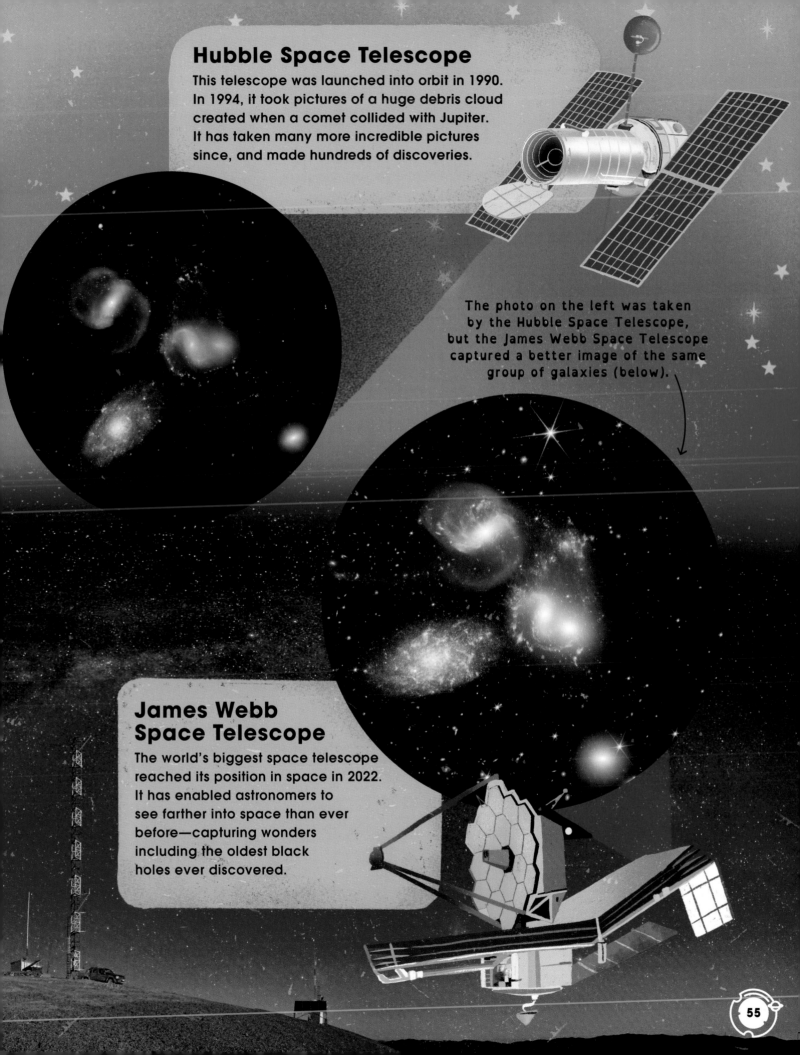

Hubble Space Telescope

This telescope was launched into orbit in 1990. In 1994, it took pictures of a huge debris cloud created when a comet collided with Jupiter. It has taken many more incredible pictures since, and made hundreds of discoveries.

The photo on the left was taken by the Hubble Space Telescope, but the James Webb Space Telescope captured a better image of the same group of galaxies (below).

James Webb Space Telescope

The world's biggest space telescope reached its position in space in 2022. It has enabled astronomers to see farther into space than ever before—capturing wonders including the oldest black holes ever discovered.

Eclipses

Every so often, the Earth, moon, and sun line up in the sky, creating eclipses. When the moon moves in between the sun and Earth, it blocks the sun's light from reaching us. We call this a solar eclipse. When the Earth blocks the sun from shining on the moon, the result is a lunar eclipse.

7.5 MIN

The longest possible duration for a total solar eclipse is 7.5 minutes.

Total solar eclipse

If the moon covers the entire disk of the sun, blocking out all of its light, some people on Earth can see a total solar eclipse.

Ring of fire

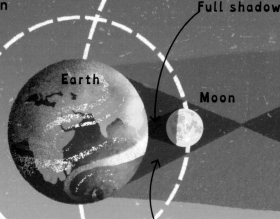

Full shadow

Earth

Moon

Partial shadow

Solar eclipse

sun

Partial solar eclipse

When the moon covers only a part of the sun's disk, blocking some of its light, this creates a partial solar eclipse.

Partial eclipse

Diamond rings

Just before and after a total solar eclipse, some sunlight can still pass through the mountains on the surface of the moon. This causes a flash called a diamond ring.

Diamond rings do not happen during every total solar eclipse. When they do, they are very bright and are over very quickly.

Partial lunar eclipse

Earth casts a shadow into space. When the moon moves into the edges of that shadow, it is called a partial lunar eclipse.

Partial lunar eclipse

Total lunar eclipse

When the moon sits in the full shadow of the Earth, it creates a total lunar eclipse. The moon is still visible on Earth, but it glows a blood-red color (see page 37).

Total lunar eclipse

Full shadow

Earth

Moon

Lunar eclipse

Partial shadow

Unhappy gods

Ancient Greeks thought that eclipses were a bad omen. They believed the gods asked the sun to abandon Earth because they had done something to anger them. The word "eclipse" means "abandonment" in Greek.

The moon's orbit

The path the moon takes around Earth is tilted compared to Earth's path around the sun. This is why we do not see an eclipse every month when the moon is in full view, since most of the time the Earth, the moon, and the sun do not line up in the sky.

Earth's axis of rotation is also tilted compared to its orbit.

Sun

Moon

Earth

Earth orbits the sun around an imaginary line in space. We only see an eclipse when the moon crosses this line.

Starry skies

Humans have been making up stories about the patterns created by stars for thousands of years. These patterns are known as constellations, and they have been given their own names based on their shape—whether that be a simple cross or a mythical beast.

Naming constellations

The ancient Greeks named many of the constellations we see today—which is why they are often named after creatures or characters from Greek myths. Today, a body of astronomers called the International Astronomical Union decides which patterns of stars become official constellations.

Northern constellations

Southern Hemisphere

Southern constellations

Southern constellations

Staring up from a point in the Earth's Southern Hemisphere, these are some of the constellations you might see.

One of the biggest constellations in the night sky, **Centaurus**, looks like a centaur—a mythical creature that is half man and half horse.

The Great Dog, **Canis Major**, is home to Sirius, the brightest star in the night sky.

The Southern Cross contains five bright stars that make a cross pattern, which points south. It is visible all year

Named after the mythical bird, **Phoenix** can't be seen from most parts of the Northern Hemisphere. It is one of three southern bird constellations.

Dorado, the dolphinfish, is also sometimes thought to look like a swordfish. It is home to the Large Magellanic Cloud, a small galaxy that orbits the Milky Way.

The peacock, **Pavo**, contains a pattern of stars called the saucepan. It can be used in the Southern Hemisphere to figure out which direction is south.

Chamaeleon, named after the lizard, is sometimes called the Frying Pan in Australia. It is one of the smallest constellations in the sky.

There are 88 officially recognized constellations.

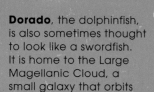

Northern constellations

As with the southern constellations, some constellations are only fully visible, or are much easier to find, in the Northern Hemisphere.

The Big Dipper

The North Star

The Great Bear, **Ursa Major,** contains a famous pattern of stars called the Big Dipper, or the Plough. Two stars in the Big Dipper point toward the North Star.

The North Star sits in the constellation **Ursa Minor**. It is called Polaris or Pole Star because it shows the direction of north.

The dragon, **Draco,** can be found very far north in the night sky. Viewed from the Northern Hemisphere, it never sets.

The W-shaped **Cassiopeia** represents a queen who was the mother of the princess Andromeda in Greek mythology.

In Greek mythology, **Cepheus** was married to Cassiopeia. The constellation sits next to Cassiopeia in the northern part of the sky.

This constellation's name, *Camelopardalis*, is Greek for "giraffe." The word comes from "camel-leopard," because a giraffe has leopardlike spots and a camel's long neck.

Northern Hemisphere

Equator

Orion

Asterisms

Patterns of stars that are not official constellations are called asterisms. Sometimes, asterisms can be made of stars from different constellations. In other cases, patterns within a bigger constellation—such as the three stars of Orion's Belt—make an asterism.

Both hemispheres

Many constellations span both hemispheres—they are fully visible from all parts of the world.

The Hunter, **Orion,** can be seen from both hemispheres. It looks like a hunter holding a sword and a shield, chasing **Taurus,** the bull constellation— which is next to it in the night sky. This constellation contains many bright stars.

Orion's Belt is made up of three supergiant stars—Alnitak, Alnilam, and Mintaka.

Mapping the sky

Constellations and other arrangements of the brightest stars can be used to make a map of the night sky. This map helps us to understand how the sky changes throughout the year.

All the stars we can see with the naked eye are in the Milky Way galaxy.

Aries
Aries represents a ram and sits in a dark, empty part of the sky.

Taurus
Taurus the bull is home to two star clusters—the Pleiades and the Hyades.

The world's oldest star map, the Nebra sky disk, could date back to 1600 BCE.

Gemini
Gemini is recognized by its bright twin stars—Castor and Pollux.

Maps of the sky

Historically, different groups of people around the world have observed star patterns and created their own maps of the sky. Sometimes they picked out the same shapes, but many of the stories and figures they linked to the stars were unique.

Cancer
The crab, Cancer, is home to a group of stars called the Beehive cluster.

Earth

Leo
Leo the lion is a constellation visible from almost anywhere on the planet.

Virgo
The word Virgo means maiden in Latin. It is the biggest of all the zodiacal constellations.

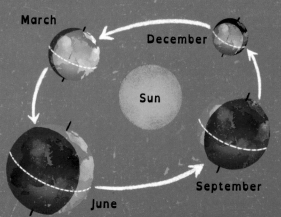

March

December

Sun

September

June

Seasonal skies

Different parts of the Earth are tilted toward or away from the hot sun at different times in its year-long orbit. This causes our seasons. The stars in the sky also appear to change with the seasons, as we face different stars at night depending on which side of the sun we are on.

The Zodiac

The zodiac is made up of 12 constellations. These are traditionally thought to be special because they move through the path the sun traces across the sky, which is called the ecliptic.

The Serpent bearer

The constellation Ophiuchus, which the ancient Greeks thought resembled a serpent bearer, is often thought to be the 13th zodiacal constellation because it also crosses the ecliptic. It is not one of the traditional constellations of the zodiac.

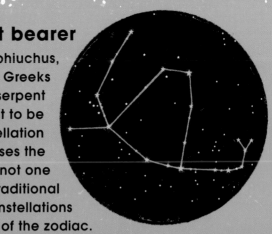

Pisces
The double fish of Pisces is one of the biggest constellations.

Aquarius
Aquarius, the Water Bearer, is the oldest of all the zodiacal constellations.

Capricorn
The constellation Capricornus represents a horned sea goat, which is half goat, half fish.

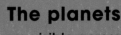

Sagittarius
The archer, Sagittarius, is one of the zodiacal constellations that sits in the Southern Hemisphere sky.

Scorpio
The constellation Scorpius represents a scorpion, and it sits near the middle of the Milky Way.

Libra
Libra, which represents weighing scales, is one of the fainter zodiacal constellations in the sky.

The planets

The easiest planets to view are visible across the early evening sky from west to southeast. Look for Venus first, then Jupiter, Saturn, and Mars, as twilight gives way to nightfall.

Mars   Moon   Saturn   Antares   Jupiter   Spica Venus

Space agencies

Organizations that work to send astronauts, spacecraft, and other objects into space are called space agencies. There are six big space agencies, funded by countries from all over the world.

There have been eight crewed missions to the moon, all by NASA in the 1960s and '70s. On six of these, astronauts landed on the moon.

NASA

The National Aeronautics and Space Administration (NASA) is the US's space agency. It was founded in 1958 and has been at the forefront of space exploration ever since. In 1969, NASA landed the first humans on the moon, and in 1975 it sent the first lander to Mars.

ESA

The European Space Agency (ESA) was set up in 1975. It is made up of 22 member countries from across Europe. Most of its astronaut activity has involved work on the International Space Station (ISS). It has also attempted crewless missions to Mars.

JAXA

The Japanese Aerospace Exploration Agency (JAXA) was founded in 2003. Its work mostly involves satellites and rockets. In 2010, the agency's *Hayabusa* mission brought back the first samples from an asteroid.

JAXA built a module on the ISS with a robotic arm, called *Kibo—w* is Japanese for "hope."

In 1983, Sally Ride became the first American woman in space.

The German astronaut Ulf Merbold was the first non-American to fly on a NASA spacecraft, and flew on two ESA missions.

International Space Station

The International Space Station (ISS) is a joint project between five different space agencies. It first went into orbit around Earth in 1998, and there have always been astronauts living aboard since 2000. Almost 300 people have lived on the space station over its lifetime.

ISRO

The Indian Space Research Organisation (ISRO) was created in 1969. It has deployed satellites, sent orbiters and landers to the moon, an orbiter to Mars, and a mission to study the sun.

RFSA

The Russian Federal Space Agency (RFSA) is also known as Roscosmos. It was founded in 1992, although Russia has been involved in space exploration since 1957, when it launched the first satellite into space—*Sputnik 1*.

CNSA

The China National Space Administration (CNSA) was set up in 1993. It was the first agency to land a craft on the far side of the moon, and in 2021 it launched its own space station, Tiangong.

The third in a series of ISRO moon missions, *Chandrayaan-3* was launched in July 2023 and is now orbiting the moon.

Russia's Valentina Tereshkova flew a solo mission in 1963 to become the first woman in space.

In 2003, Yang Liwei was the first person to be sent to space by CNSA.

Space heroes

Astronauts are the first people that spring to mind when we think of space exploration, but space missions would not be possible without hundreds of people playing many different roles. They include engineers, mathematicians, and scientists, who help design missions, study data collected by spacecraft, and much more.

Nearly half a million people worked on the Apollo missions!

Ground control

Mission controllers are experts on the ground who communicate with the spacecraft, or with the astronauts onboard if it is a crewed mission. They help control the spacecraft and make sure that it completes its mission safely.

This picture shows ground controllers watching the space walk by *Apollo 15* command module pilot Alfred M. Worden, in 1971.

Astronauts

Astronauts are the people who go into space. Since the 1970s, most astronauts have only traveled as far as Earth's orbit, on spacecraft such as the International Space Station.

Astronauts collecting moon rocks

In 1958, Mary Jackson became the first black female engineer to work for NASA.

Engineers

Engineers design and build the rockets that send spacecraft out of Earth's atmosphere. They also design the spacecraft themselves, including all the instruments and computers onboard.

Programmers

Computers are needed for every part of a space mission—including controlling the spacecraft. Programmers design and maintain the software that enables space missions to take place.

Margaret Hamilton was in charge of the team that developed the software for the *Apollo* moon missions.

Mathematicians

Many jobs in space agencies require complex math. Mathematicians are vital for helping engineers design missions. One of their key roles is calculating the path that space missions will take.

Katherine Johnson calculated the paths of many of the first space flights, including missions to the moon.

The Mars Exploration Rover mission landed two rovers, *Spirit* and *Opportunity*, on the red planet.

Robotic missions

Much of space exploration involves sending robots and rovers into space instead of humans. But there are always people back on Earth constantly monitoring the craft and giving them instructions.

The space race

During the 1950s, '60s, and '70s, a great rivalry began between the US and the Soviet Union (now Russia). The nations were in competition to be the best at crewed space exploration. The Soviet Union seemed to be winning at first, but the US was the first to send people to the moon.

1 Sputnik 1

The first satellite launched into orbit around Earth was *Sputnik 1*, in 1975. The piece of metal was just 23 in (58 cm) across, but it could transmit radio signals. This event started the space race, and took the Soviet Union into the lead.

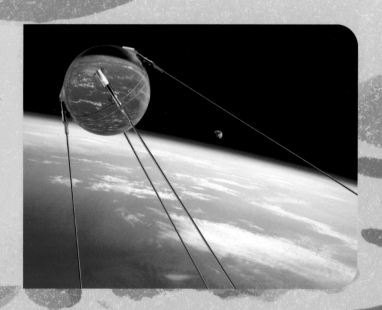

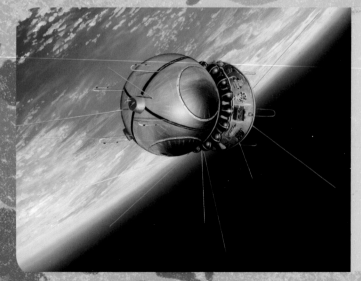

2 Vostok 1

The first human to reach space, Yuri Gagarin, went into orbit on a spacecraft called *Vostok 1* in April 1961. The Soviet astronaut spent 108 minutes in space, before returning in a capsule and parachuting back to the ground from 4.3 miles (7 km) above Earth.

Where's the fruit?

The first animals sent into space were fruit flies!

Animals in space

A lot of animals, including monkeys, dogs, mice, rabbits and spiders, have been sent into space. The first dog in space, Laika, was sent up by the Soviet Union in 1957.

3 **Mercury-Redstone 3**
Alan Shepard was the first US astronaut to go into space. His successful mission on the *Mercury-Redstone 3* took place in May 1961, just a few weeks after *Vostok 1*.

Walking on the moon

From 1969 to 1972, 12 people have set foot on the moon as part of six separate Apollo missions. NASA is planning to send more people back to the moon, in a mission called Artemis.

4 **Apollo 11**
The space race ended with US victory in July 1969 when NASA sent two people, Neil Armstrong and Buzz Aldrin, to walk on the moon for the first time. The third member of the *Apollo 11* mission, Michael Collins, remained in the spacecraft.

Mars missions

Exploring Mars is tricky. Since 1971, there have been 20 attempts to land robots on the red planet—and 11 of these either crashed, were damaged soon after landing, or missed the planet entirely. Those missions that made it, however, have sent back amazing photos and findings from the surface.

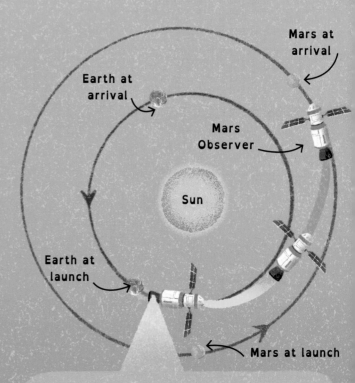

Mars at arrival

Earth at arrival

Mars Observer

Sun

Earth at launch

Mars at launch

Orbiting Mars

Getting into orbit around Mars requires perfect timing. Mars missions are planned years in advance, and launch windows are based on the orbits of Earth and Mars around the sun.

Airbags of Mars Pathfinder

The first rover

The first Mars rover was a 22-lb (10-kg) NASA robot named *Sojourner*, which was part of the Pathfinder mission. After landing successfully on the Martian surface in 1997, it operated for 92 Martian days.

Sojourner rover

Rosalind Franklin rover

The *Rosalind Franklin* rover, which used to be called *ExoMars*, is a planned mission led by the European Space Agency to land a rover on Mars in 2029.

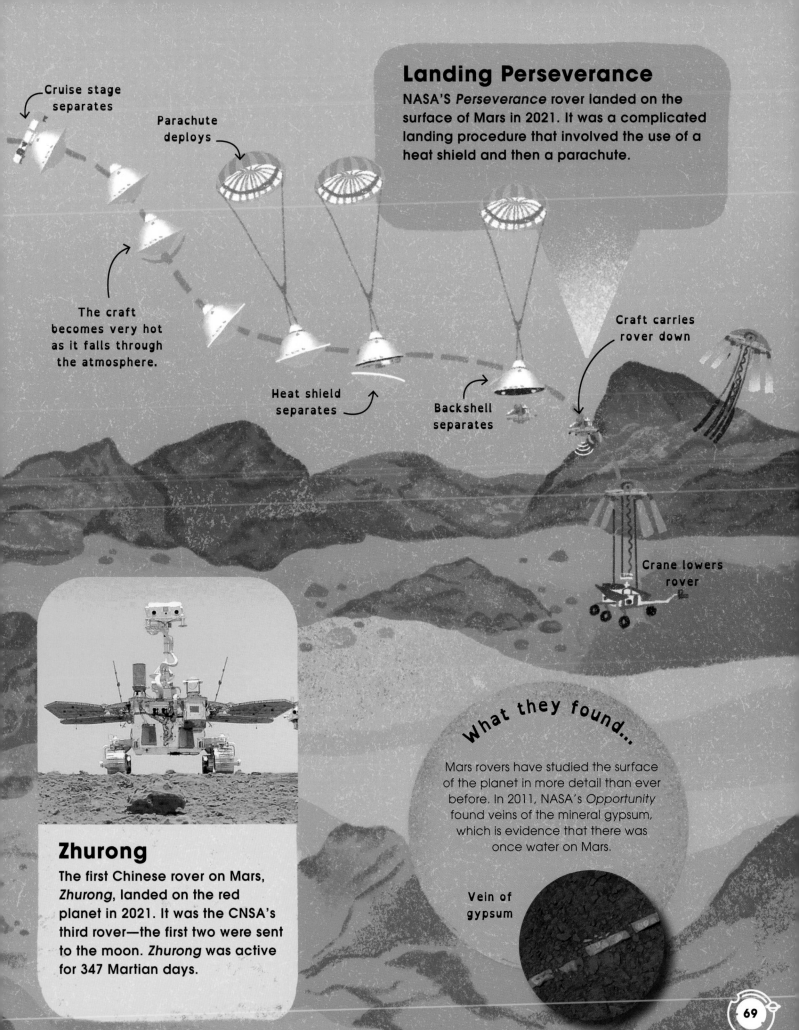

Cruise stage
separates

Parachute
deploys

Landing Perseverance

NASA'S *Perseverance* rover landed on the surface of Mars in 2021. It was a complicated landing procedure that involved the use of a heat shield and then a parachute.

The craft
becomes very hot
as it falls through
the atmosphere.

Craft carries
rover down

Heat shield
separates

Backshell
separates

Crane lowers
rover

What they found...

Mars rovers have studied the surface of the planet in more detail than ever before. In 2011, NASA's *Opportunity* found veins of the mineral gypsum, which is evidence that there was once water on Mars.

Zhurong

The first Chinese rover on Mars, *Zhurong*, landed on the red planet in 2021. It was the CNSA's third rover—the first two were sent to the moon. *Zhurong* was active for 347 Martian days.

Vein of
gypsum

Moving to Mars

Earth is the perfect place for humans—it has water to drink, the right amount of heat, air with enough oxygen to breathe, and an atmosphere that protects us from harmful space radiation. We would need to protect ourselves from much harsher conditions if we were to live on other planets, such as Mars.

Ganymede

Europa

Callisto

Titan

Farther afield

Some of the moons of gas giants could, one day, provide the right conditions for life. Saturn's moon Titan has a weather system, and some of Jupiter's moons have underground oceans.

Mars

68°F
(20°C)

–243°F
(–153°C)

Temperatures

The temperature on other planets is very different from that on Earth. Because Mars is farther away from the sun, the temperature can drop to –243°F (–153°C) at night.

Extreme temperatures and a lack of oxygen would mean the need for protective suits with oxygen tanks.

Growing food

Plants need oxygen, liquid water, and soil with channels created by insects for water to flow through—none of which exist on Mars. These conditions would need to be created in special, protective buildings for plants to grow.

Oxygen would need to be pumped into buildings.

Solar panels could create electricity.

Surface of Mars

Since the moon is much closer to us than Mars, building a space station there would be simpler! But, like Mars, there is a very thin atmosphere, and no water or suitable soil for plants—so we would need similar suits and buildings.

No air

The lack of atmosphere on Mars means humans could never go outside without wearing a space suit. There is no oxygen to breathe, or any protection from the sun's harmful radiation. Space rocks also rain down constantly, since there is no atmosphere to break them apart.

Gravity

The gravity on Mars is just under half the strength of gravity on Earth, so walking around would feel very different. You could take much bigger steps and jump much higher. Walking would also be much slower on the red planet.

Houses could be 3D printed on the surface.

It is easier to walk on Mars than on the moon since Mars has more gravity.

Greenhouses would need to create the right conditions for plants.

Space junk

Since *Sputnik 1* launched in 1957, tens of thousands of satellites have been sent into space. Many of these have stopped working and are now littering Earth's orbit, broken into what we call space junk.

Paint flecks

Although they are tiny, pieces of paint that have flaked off spacecraft can be extremely dangerous. They move so fast that they can damage satellites or spacecraft if they hit them— which happened to the ISS in 2016.

Dead satellites

Many broken satellites create larger pieces of space junk. There are believed to be more than 3,000 dead satellites orbiting Earth. This contributes to the thousands of tons of space junk.

Sputnik

Collisions

With so many pieces of debris in orbit, avoiding a collision can be difficult for spacecraft. With the pieces of junk moving at such high speeds, even small impacts can be dangerous.

Getting back

Some pieces of space junk are far away enough from Earth that they stay in orbit for years. Others fall into Earth's atmosphere and, like meteorites, burn up as they reenter.

Larger pieces of space junk are sometimes brought back to Earth on purpose. One example is the ESA's *Jules Verne*, a cargo vehicle that supplied the ISS. It was deliberately destroyed by guiding it back to Earth in 2008.

Kessler Syndrome

When space junk collides, more pieces of junk are created, which could collide to create more junk... Eventually, this could make Earth's orbit too dangerous for satellites or spacecraft, in an effect called the Kessler Syndrome.

Removing the junk

Space junk is a huge problem, and it is not easy to fix. This is why space agencies across the world are looking for ways to clean up the space surrounding our planet.

A mission called RemoveDEBRIS was deployed in 2018 to try out different ways of removing pieces of space junk.

Future exploration

Our missions into space and powerful telescopes have given us great knowledge about the solar system, galaxies, and the distant universe. Yet there is still so much more to learn— and for that we need new space missions. Here are a few of the upcoming projects to get excited about.

Hera will study the crater made by the DART collision.

Hera

Hera is an ESA mission planned to launch in October 2024. It will visit the asteroid Didymos, to study the effects of a NASA mission from 2022 called DART, which deliberately crashed a spacecraft into the asteroid to alter its orbit.

The telescope is set to begin observing the sky in 2025.

Vera Rubin Observatory

The Vera Rubin Observatory is a telescope being built on a mountain in the north of Chile. It will continuously scan the entire southern hemisphere sky for 330 nights a year over a period of ten years.

Solar power in space

Space agencies think that placing solar panels in space and beaming the energy back to Earth could be a way of providing us with renewable energy. The ESA is working on such a project, called Solaris.

It is never cloudy in space, so solar panels will always work as long as they are facing the sun.

LISA

NASA and ESA are planning a joint project to build an observatory in space. Called the Laser Interferometer Space Antenna (LISA), it will detect minuscule ripples in space-time called gravitational waves. The launch is planned for 2035.

This drawing shows what LISA will look like when it is in space.

Gateway

Many space agencies want to one day have a space station like the ISS in place around the moon, to help launch missions to Mars. NASA is building the space station Gateway, which it is aiming to launch in 2025.

Artemis

As part of its Artemis mission, NASA is planning to send the first woman and the first person of color to the moon. The first crewed launches are planned for the late 2020s.

GLOSSARY

asteroid
Rocky object that orbits the sun and is smaller than a dwarf planet

astronaut
Person whose job is to travel into space

astronomer
Person who studies space

atmosphere
Layer of gases around a planet or moon

atom
Particle that makes up everything in the universe

black hole
Area in space with a very strong gravitational pull, created when a star collapses

carbon
Element that can be found in a lot of objects and living things in the universe

celestial object
Object in space

comet
Object made of ice and dust that orbits the sun

compound
Substance made up of two elements or more

constellation
Group of stars that form a dot-to-dot pattern

crater
Hole in the surface of a space object, such as a planet, created when another space object crashed into it

debris
Pieces remaining from an object that has been destroyed

element
Substance that cannot be broken down into other substances

ESA
European Space Agency—European organization that plans space exploration

exoplanet
Planet that orbits a star other than our sun

galaxy
Large group of stars

gas giant
Large planet made mostly of gas

gravity
Force that pulls objects toward each other

ISS
International Space Station—laboratory that orbits Earth, crewed by astronauts

light year
Distance light travels in a year

lunar
Relating to the moon

lunar eclipse
When the Earth moves between the sun and moon, blocking the sun's light from reaching the moon's surface

magnetic field
Zone around a magnet, such as the Earth, that affects other magnets or magnetic objects

matter
Physical substance, such as a solid planet

moon

Natural object that orbits a planet or asteroid

NASA

National Aeronautics and Space Administration—US agency that studies space and plans space exploration

nebula

Cloud of gas and dust in space

neutron

Particle found inside atoms

observatory

Building from which people can study space, using equipment such as telescopes

orbit

Object's path around another object in space, such as the moon's path around Earth

particle

Tiny building block that forms part of an object or a bigger particle

planet

Large, spherical object that orbits a star

reaction

Process of two substances combining to form a new substance

rocky planet

Planet made up of rock

rover

Wheeled craft that can explore a planet or moon's surface

satellite

Object that orbits another object in space

solar eclipse

When the moon moves between the sun and Earth, blocking the sun's light from reaching the Earth's surface

spacecraft

Craft used for exploring space

star

Large sphere of gas that glows, such as the sun

star cluster

Group of stars

telescope

Piece of equipment used to study space

total eclipse

When an object in space is completely in the shadow of another object

water vapor

Gas form of water

Index

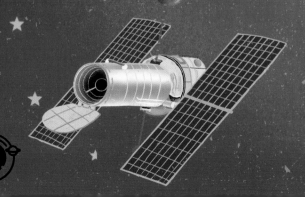

ACKNOWLEDGEMENTS

DK would like to thank Helen Peters for the index;
Polly Goodman for proofreading; and Sif Nørskov
and Charlotte Jennings for their design assistance.

The publisher would like to thank the following for their
kind permission to reproduce their photographs:

(Key: a-above; b-below/bottom; c-centre; f-far; l-left; r-right; t-top)

6-7 Dorling Kindersley: © Dawn Cooper, 20**. **8-9 Dorling Kindersley:** © Dawn Cooper, 20**. 8 ESA: NASA, ESA, CSA, J. Diego (Instituto de Física de Cantabria), B. Frye (University of Arizona), P. Kamieneski (Arizona State University), T. Carleton (Arizona State University), and R. Windhorst (University of Arizona), A. Pagan (STScI), J. Summers (Arizona State University), J. DSilva (University of Western Australia), A. Koekemoer (STScI), A. Robotham (University of Western Australia), and R. Windhorst (University of Arizona) (br). **10-11 Dorling Kindersley:** © Dawn Cooper, 20**. **11 ESA:** ESA and the Planck Collaboration (clb). **12-13 Dorling Kindersley:** © Dawn Cooper, 20**. **12 ESA:** NASA / JPL / Univ. of Arizona (fcrb). **ESO:** ESO / ALMA (ESO / NAOJ / NRAO) / Weber et al. (cb). **NASA:** NASA / ESA, R. Soummer, Ann Feild (STScI) (crb). **14-15 Dorling Kindersley:** © Dawn Cooper, 20**. **14 ESA:** NASA, ESA, CSA, and STScI, J. DePasquale (STScI); CC BY 4.0 (cl). ESO: ESO (br). **15 ESA:** NASA, ESA, CSA, and STScI, J. DePasquale (STScI) (tr). **NASA:** NASA, ESA, and E. Sabbi (ESA / STScI) (ca). **16-17 Dorling Kindersley:** © Dawn Cooper, 20**. **16 ESA:** NASA, ESA, CSA, STScI, D. Milisavljevic (Purdue University), T. Temim (Princeton University), I. De Looze (University of Gent) (bl). **17 ESA:** NASA / CXC / ASU / J. Hester et al., HST / ASU / J. Hester et al. (tc). **18-19 Dorling Kindersley:** © Dawn Cooper, 20** (BG1). **18 Alamy Stock Photo:** Stocktrek Images, Inc. (cl). **ESA / Hubble:** Davide De Martin & the ESA / ESO / NASA Photoshop FITS Liberator (cra); NASA, ESA, and STScI. (bl). **19 Alamy Stock Photo:** Stocktrek Images / Robert Gendler (crb). **ESO:** ESO / INAF-VST / OmegaCAM. Acknowledgement: A. Grado, L. Limatola / INAF-Capodimonte Observatory (cra). **20-21 Dorling Kindersley:** © Dawn Cooper, 20** (BG). **Science Photo Library:** Robert Gendler (BG1). **20 NASA:** NASA / STScI Digitized Sky Survey / Noel Carboni (cla). **Shutterstock.com:** Lukasz Pawel Szczepanski (br). **21 ESA:** ESA / Webb, NASA, CSA, M. Barlow, N. Cox, R. Wesson (cra). **NASA:** NASA, ESA, and the Hubble Heritage Team (STScI / AURA) (cb). **22-23 Dorling Kindersley:** © Dawn Cooper, 20**. **24-25 Dorling Kindersley:** Dawn Cooper (BG). **24 ESA / Hubble:** NASA, ESA, and the Hubble Heritage Team (STScI / AURA) (cl); **NASA, ESA, the Hubble Heritage Team (STScI / AURA),** J. Blakeslee (NRC Herzberg Astrophysics Program, Dominion Astrophysical Observatory), and H. Ford (JHU) (br). **ESO:** ESO / PESSTO / S. Smartt (cr). 25 ESA: ESA / Hubble & NASA; CC BY 4.0 (bc). **NASA and The Hubble Heritage Team (AURA/STScI):** NASA, ESA, and The Hubble Heritage Team (STScI / AURA); (cr). **NASA:** ESA / Hubble & NASA; Acknowledgement: Judy Schmidt (tl). **26 Science Photo Library:** Jeff Dai (cla). 26-27 Dorling Kindersley: © Dawn Cooper, 20** (BG, BG1). **28-29 Dorling Kindersley:** © Dawn Cooper, 20**. **30-31 Dorling Kindersley:** © Dawn Cooper, 20**. **32-33 Dorling Kindersley:** © Dawn Cooper, 20**. **34-35 Dorling Kindersley:** © Dawn Cooper, 20**. **35 Alamy Stock Photo:** Scott Sady / Tahoelight.com (br). **US National Science Foundation:** AURA / NSF (crb). **36-37 Alamy Stock Photo:** Brian Kushner. Dorling Kindersley: © Dawn Cooper, 20** (BG). **36 NASA:** LROC (cra, cla). **37 Alamy Stock Photo:** NASA Image Collection (cb). **Apollo Archive:** Apollo Archive / research: Danny Caes (cl). **ESA:** ESA / CESAR; M. Pérez Ayúcar; M. Castillo; M. Breitfellner (bl). **38-39 Dorling Kindersley:** © Dawn Cooper, 20**. **40-41 Dorling Kindersley:** © Dawn Cooper, 20**. **40 NASA:** JPL (ca); NASA / JPL-Caltech / UCLA / MPS / DLR / IDA (bl, bc); NASA / Johns Hopkins University Applied Physics Laboratory / Carnegie Institution of Washington (cla). **41 NASA and The Hubble Heritage Team (AURA/STScI):** NASA, James Bell (Cornell Univ.), Michael Wolff (Space Science Inst.), and The Hubble Heritage Team (STScI / AURA) (cra). NASA: (cla). **42-43 Dorling Kindersley:** Dawn Cooper (BG); © Dawn Cooper, 20** (BG1). **NASA:** JPL-Caltech / Space Science Institute (b). NASA, ESA, Jupiter ERS Team; image processing by Ricardo Hueso (UPV / EHU) and Judy Schmidt (cl). **43 NASA:** JPL / DLR (ca); JPL-Caltech / Space Science Institute (c). **44-45 Dorling Kindersley:** © Dawn Cooper, 20**. **44 NASA and The Hubble Heritage Team (AURA/STScI):** NASA, ESA, and J. Nichols (University of Leicester); (cra). NASA: JPL / MSSS (tl). **45 NASA:** JPL-Caltech / University of Arizona / University of Idaho (tl); NASAs Goddard Space Flight Center / Chris Smith (KRBwyle) (cra). **46-47 Dorling Kindersley:** © Dawn Cooper, 20**. **46 Alamy Stock Photo:** Imaginechina-Tuchong (cla). **Science Photo Library:** Dr Juerg Alean (bc). **47 Alamy Stock Photo:** Natural History Museum (fbr); Susan E. Degginger (bc). **Shutterstock.com:** Matteo Chinellato (br). **48-49 Dorling Kindersley:** © Dawn Cooper, 20**. 48 NASA: Johns Hopkins University Applied Physics Laboratory / Southwest Research Institute (cl); NASA Visualization Technology Applications And Development (VTAD) (fbr, br, bc, bl). **49 NASA and The Hubble Heritage Team (AURA/STScI):** NASA, ESA, and J. Zachary and S. Redfield (Wesleyan University); (cra). **50 Dorling Kindersley:** © Dawn Cooper, 20** (br, br/orbit). **50-51 Dorling Kindersley:** Dawn Cooper. 51 NASA: JPL-Caltech / Ames (tc). **52-53 Dorling Kindersley:** © Dawn Cooper, 20**. **54-55 Dorling Kindersley:** © Dawn Cooper, 20** (BG, BG1). **ESO:** ESO / S. Brunier. **54 Alamy Stock Photo:** Image Source Limited / Victoria Zeffert (bc); IMAGO / Ou Dongqu (c). **55 NASA and The Hubble Heritage Team (AURA/STScI):** NASA, ESA, and G. Bacon, J. DePasquale, F. Summers, and Z. Levay (STScI); (ca). **NASA:** ESA, CSA, STScI (crb). **56-57 Dorling Kindersley:** © Dawn Cooper, 20**. **56 NASA:** Keegan Barber (cl); Carla Thomas (bc); Norah Moran / Johnson Space Center (cb). **57 NASA:** Joel Kowsky (tc); JSC (cla). **58-59 Dorling Kindersley:** © Dawn Cooper, 20** (BG, BG1). **59 Alamy Stock Photo:** Stocktrek Images, Inc. / Alan Dyer (br). **60 Alamy Stock Photo:** dpa picture alliance / Soeren Stache (cla). **60-61 Dorling Kindersley:** © Dawn Cooper, 20** (BG, BG1). 62 NASA: (crb). **62-63 Dorling Kindersley:** © Dawn Cooper, 20**. **63 Alamy Stock Photo:** UPI (clb). **NASA:** NASA (S132-E-012208) (tr). **64-65 Dorling Kindersley:** © Dawn Cooper, 20** (BG, BG1). 64 Alamy Stock Photo: Associated Press (ca). **NASA:** (cla). **65 Alamy Stock Photo:** Science History Images (cra). **NASA:** NASA Langley Research CenterCaption text: Margot Lee Shetterly (tl); NASA Langley Research Center (clb). **66 Science Photo Library:** Richard Bizley (clb); Detlev Van Ravenswaay (cra). **66-67 Dorling Kindersley:** © Dawn Cooper, 20** (BG, BG1). 67 **Shutterstock.com:** Ralph Morse / The LIFE Picture Collection / Shutterstock (cr). **68-69 Dorling Kindersley:** © Dawn Cooper, 20**. 68 ESA: ESA / Mlabspace (crb). **Science Photo Library:** Detlev Van Ravenswaay (cl). **69 Alamy Stock Photo:** Xinhua (clb). **NASA:** JPL-Caltech / Cornell / ASU (br). **70-71 Dorling Kindersley:** © Dawn Cooper, 20**. 70 NASA: JPL / University of Arizona / University of Idaho (ca); JPL / DLR (cr/Callisto, cra, ca/Ganymede). **71 Dorling Kindersley:** © Dawn Cooper, 20** (cr). **Getty Images / iStock:** dottedhippo (tl); E+ / gremlin (cra). **72 Dorling Kindersley:** © Dawn Cooper, 20** (cl). **Dreamstime.com:** Vitalii Gaydukov (clb). Shutterstock.com: Paul Fleet (br). **72-73 Dorling Kindersley:** © Dawn Cooper, 20** (Background). **73 NASA:** ESA / Bill Moede and Jesse Carpenter (tc); JSC / Drew Feustel (br). **74 Alamy Stock Photo:** Science Photo Library / Mark Garlick (crb). **ESA:** ESA / Space Safety / Hera (tr). NOIRLab: Rubin Observatory / NOIRLab / NSF / AURA / B. Quint (cl). **74-75 Dorling Kindersley:** © Dawn Cooper, 20**. **75 Alamy Stock Photo:** NASA Photo (c)

Cover images: Spine: NASA: Johns Hopkins University Applied Physics Laboratory / Carnegie Institution of Washington ca

All other images © Dorling Kindersley Limited